The Ugly Duckling

Story by Teresa Heapy

Illustrated by Adam Record

OXFORD
UNIVERSITY PRESS

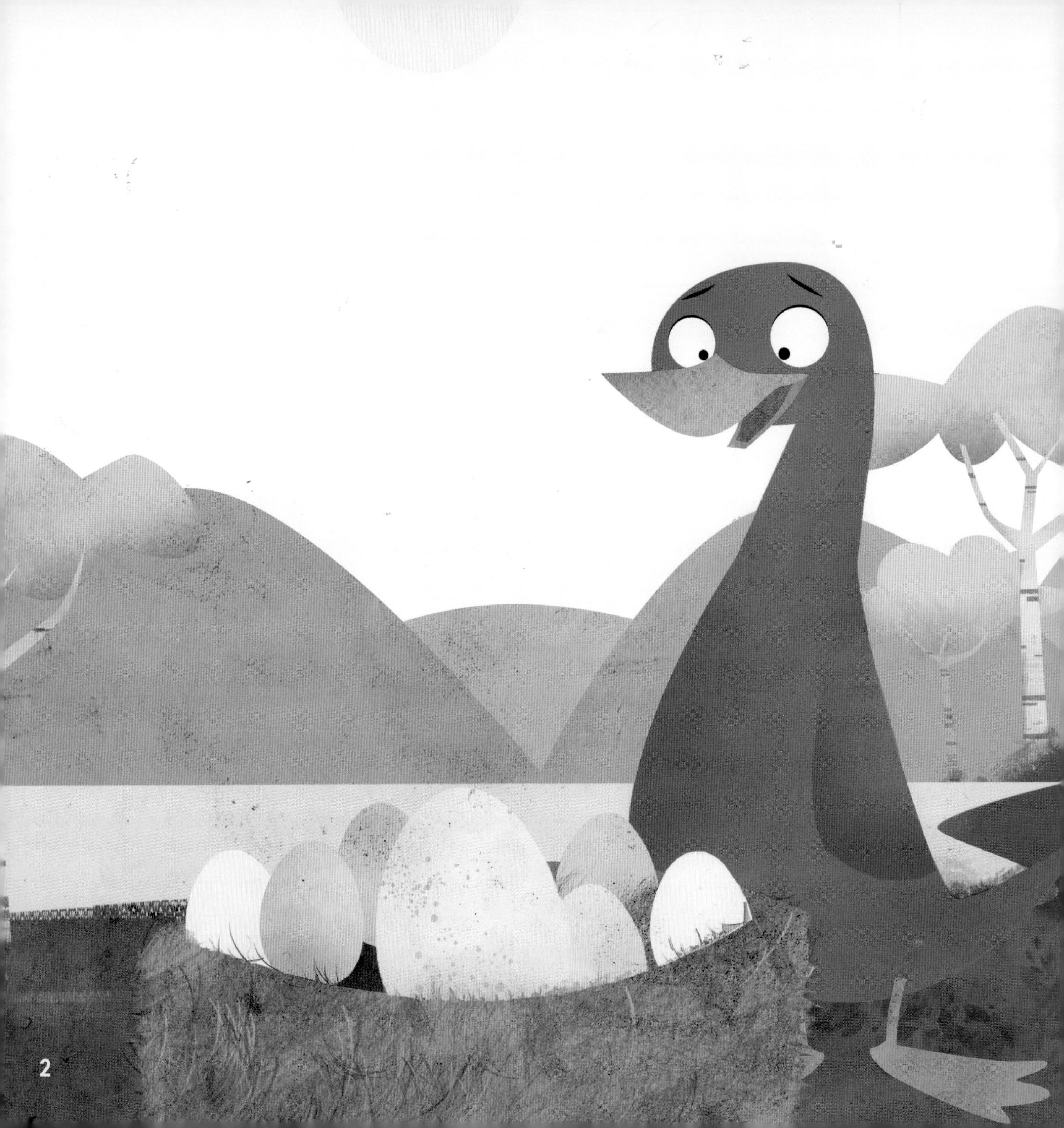

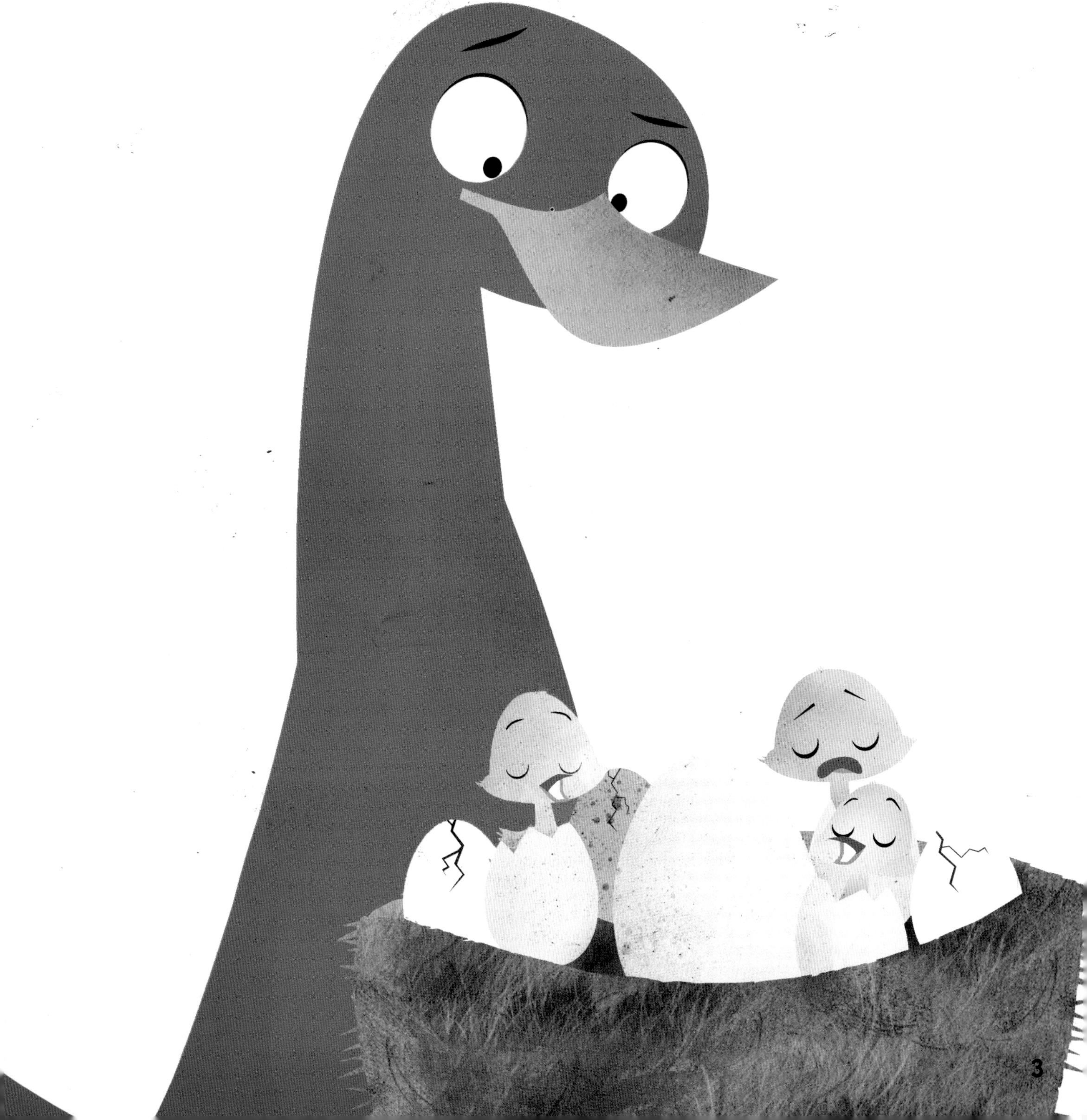

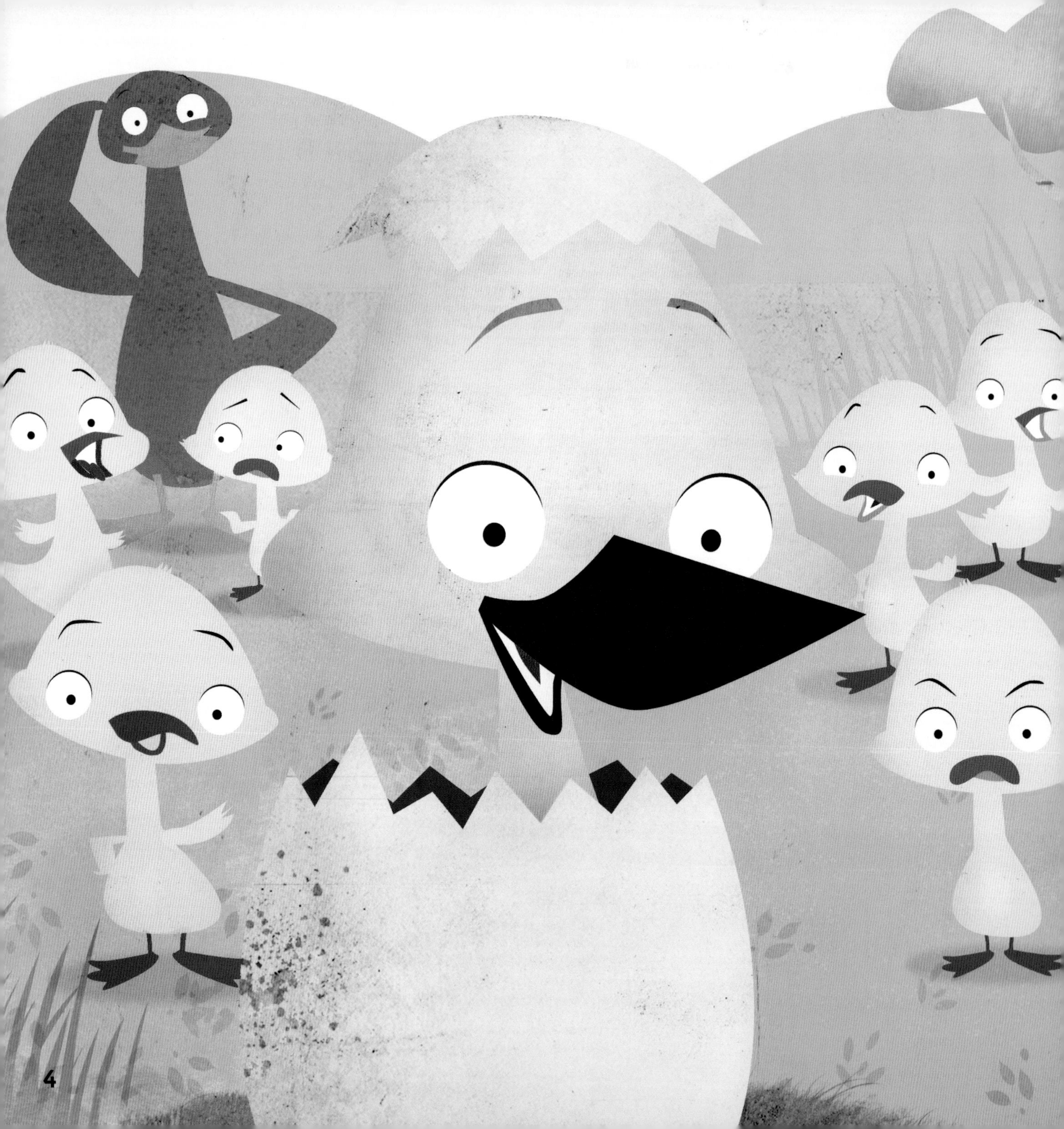

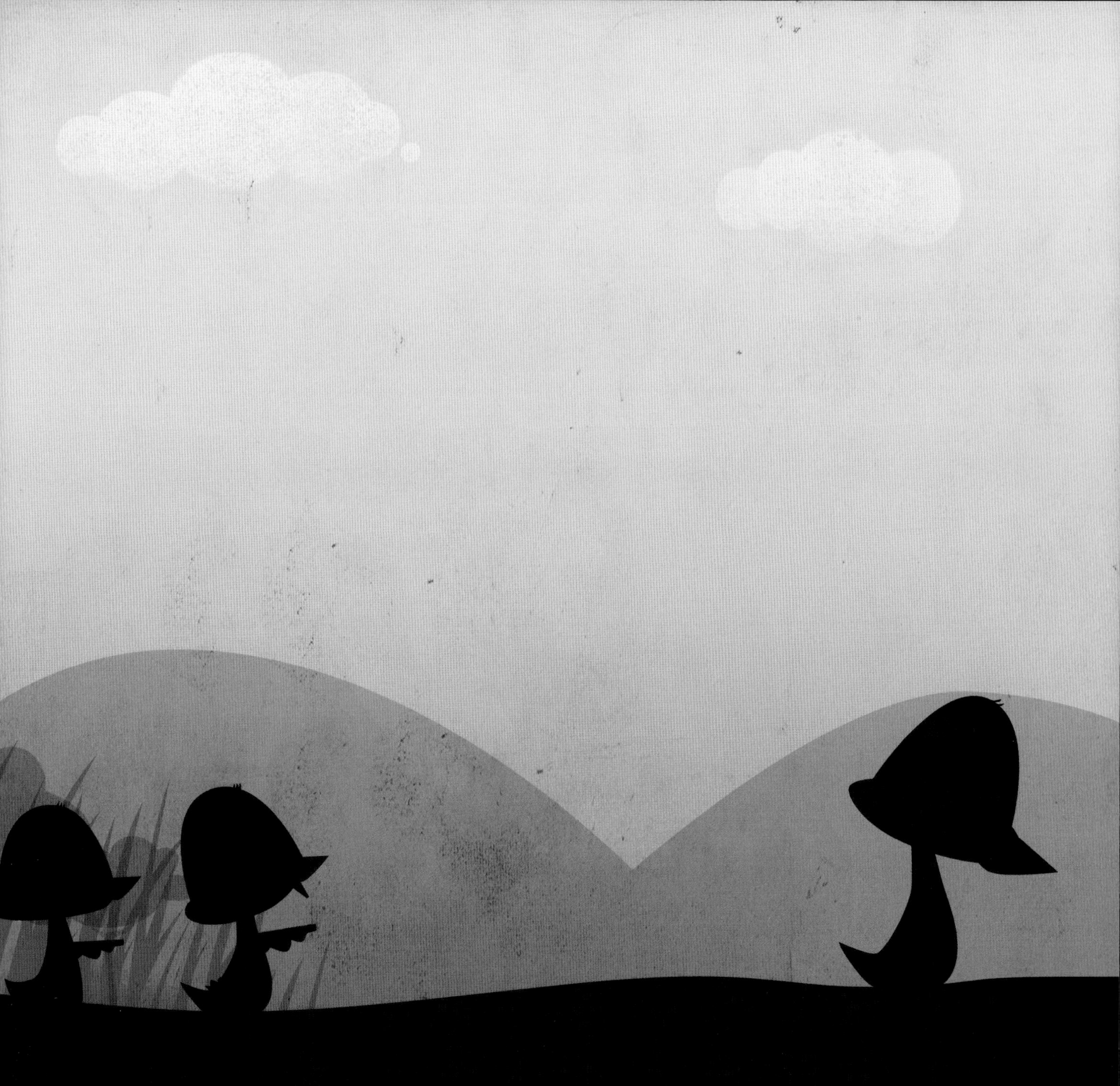

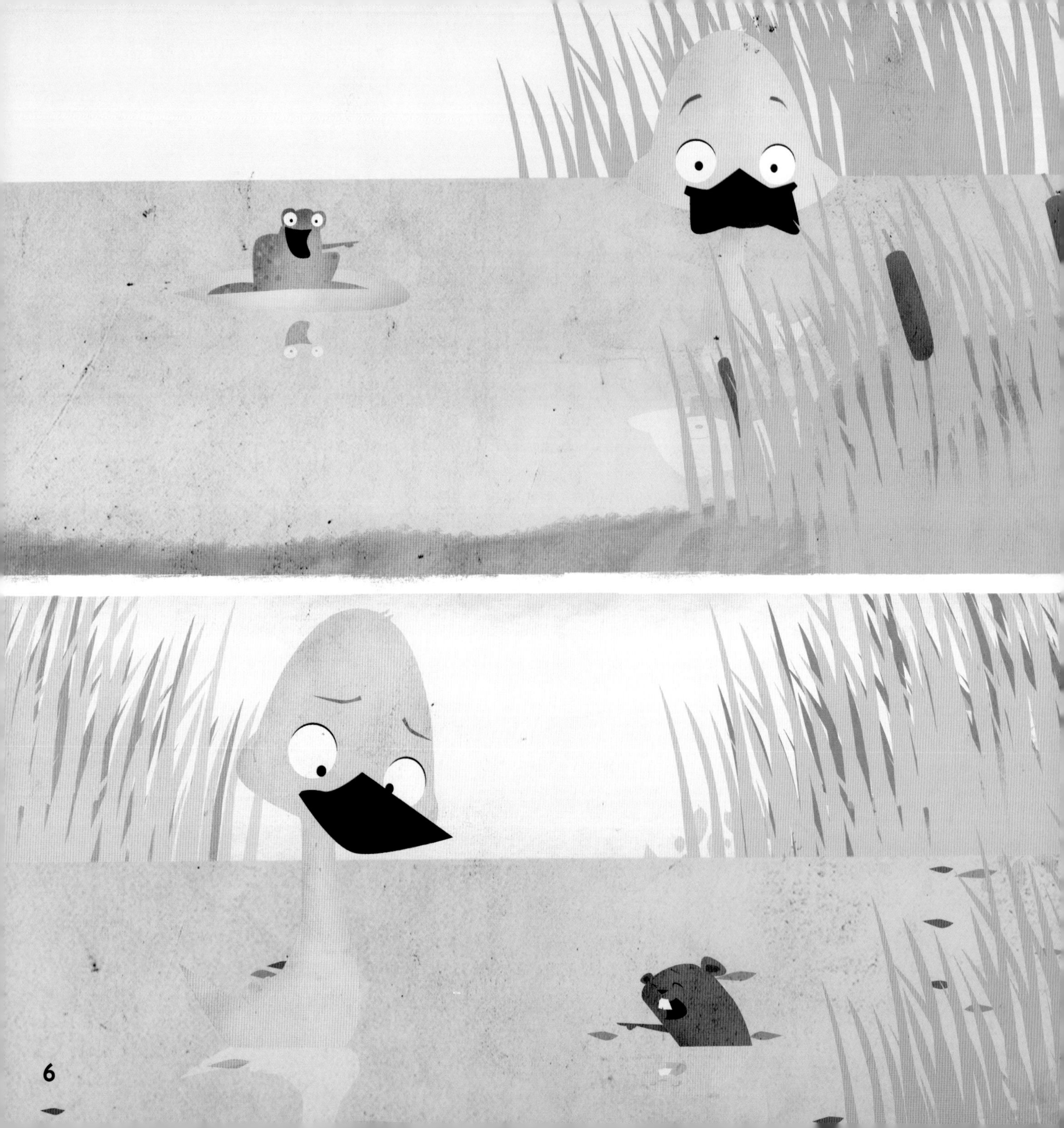

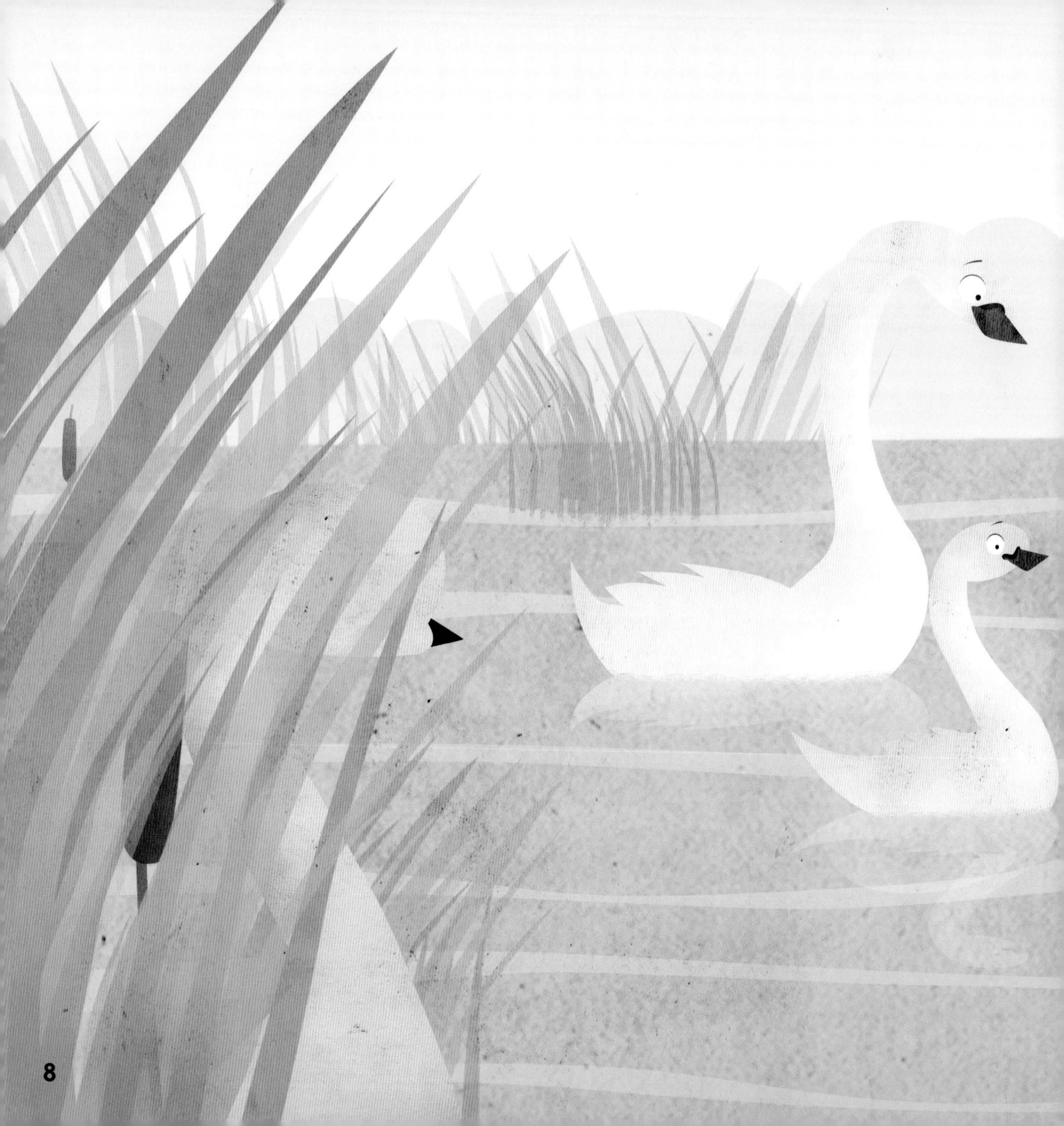

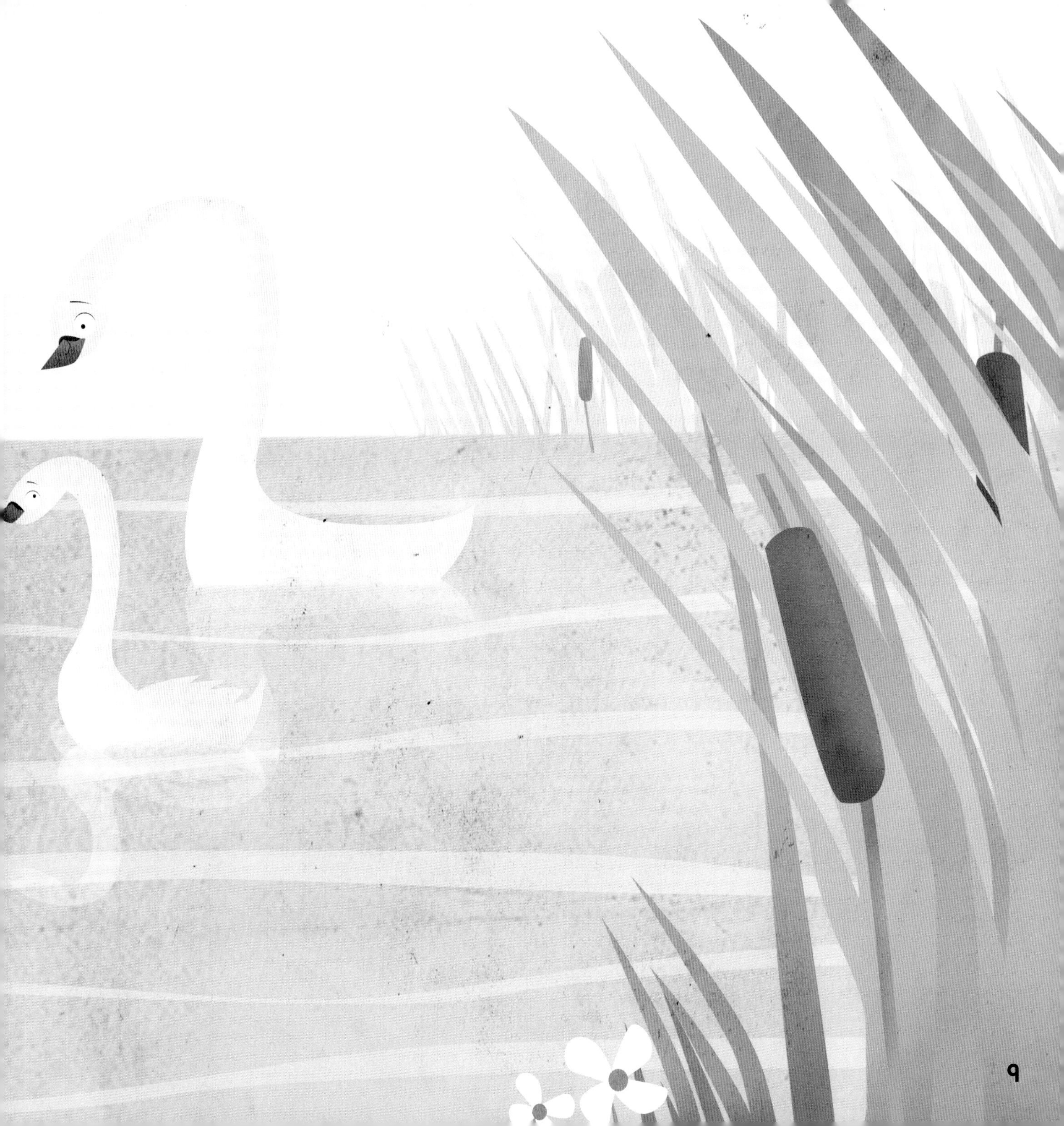

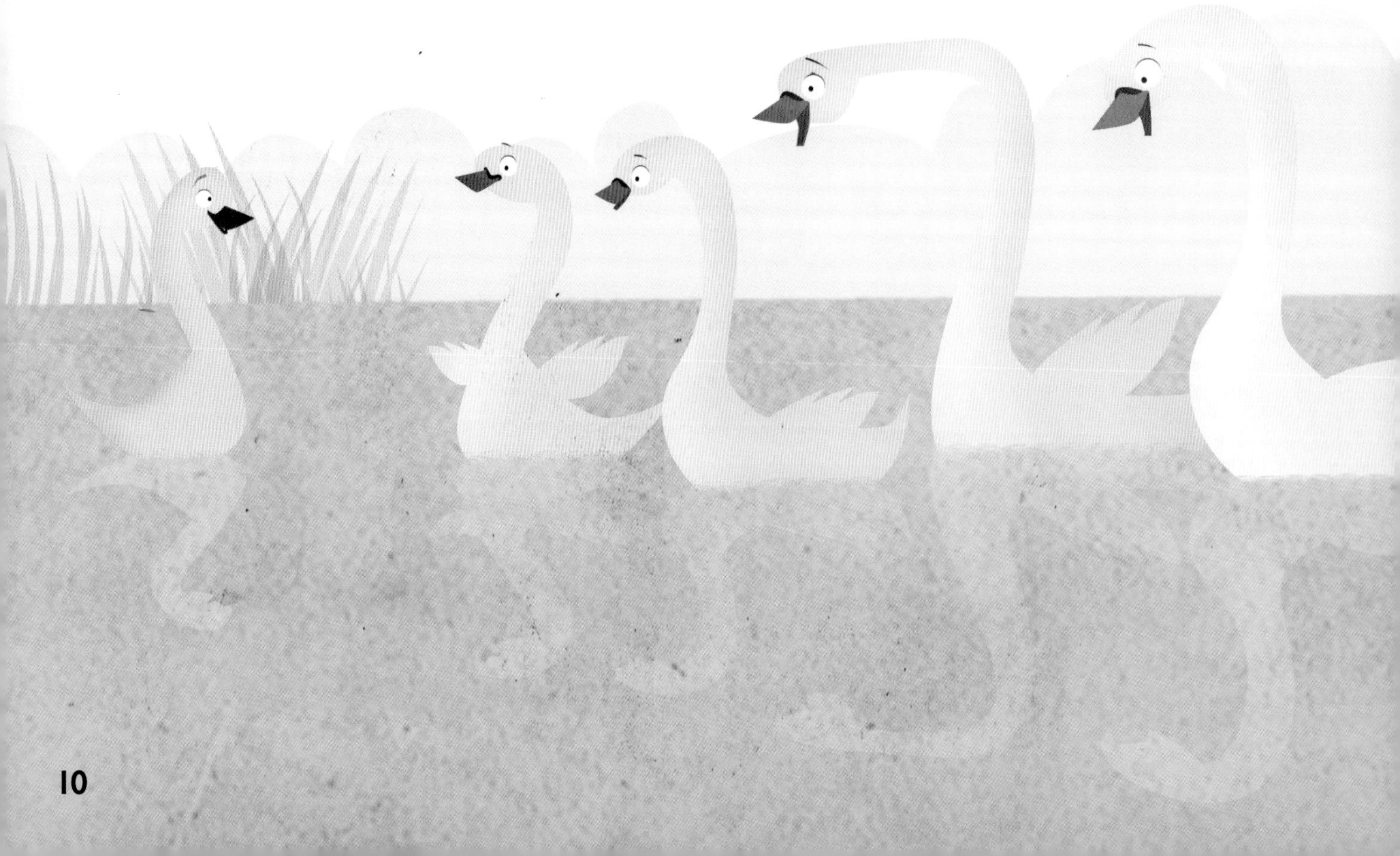

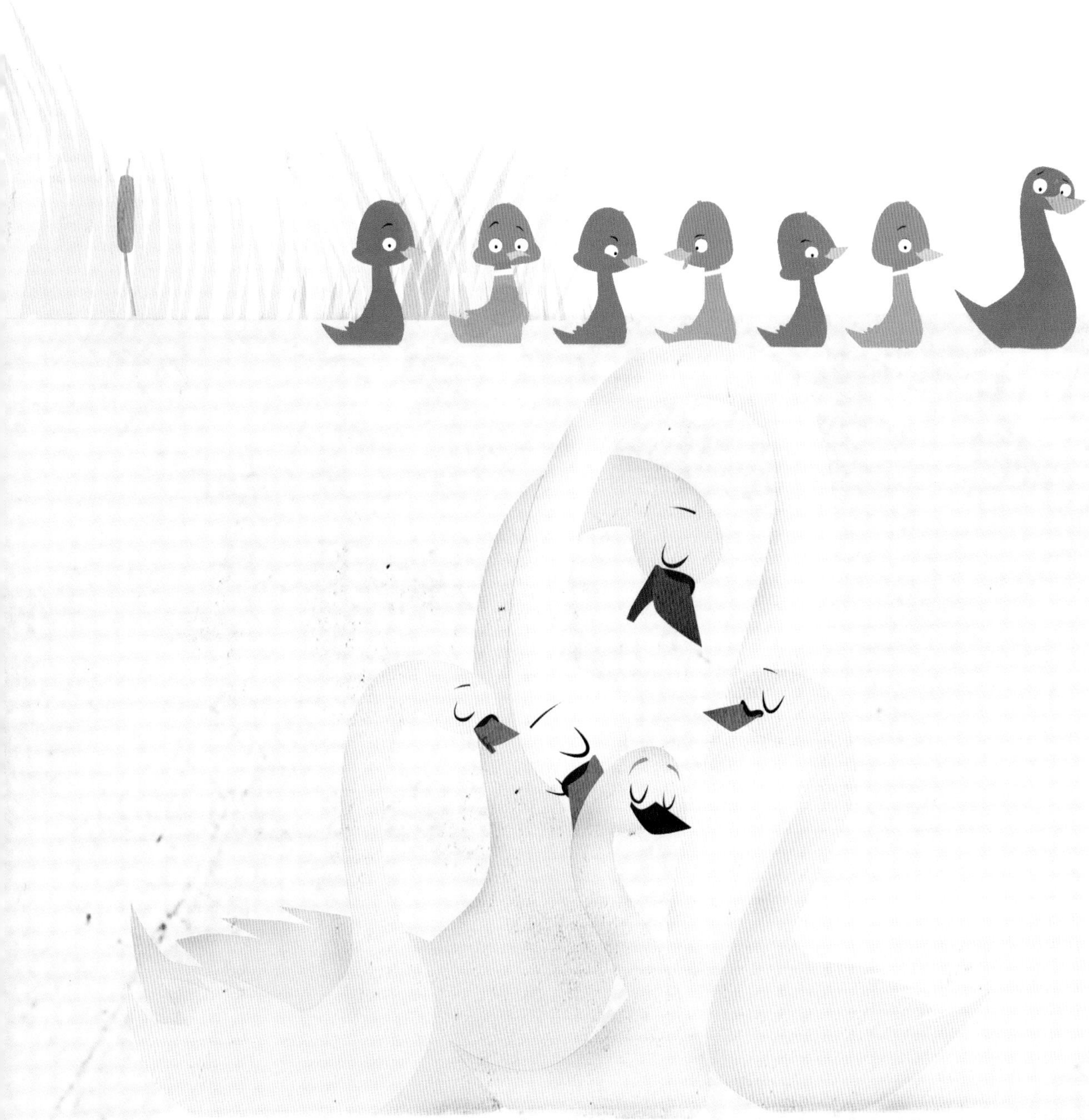

Retell the story

Once upon a time...

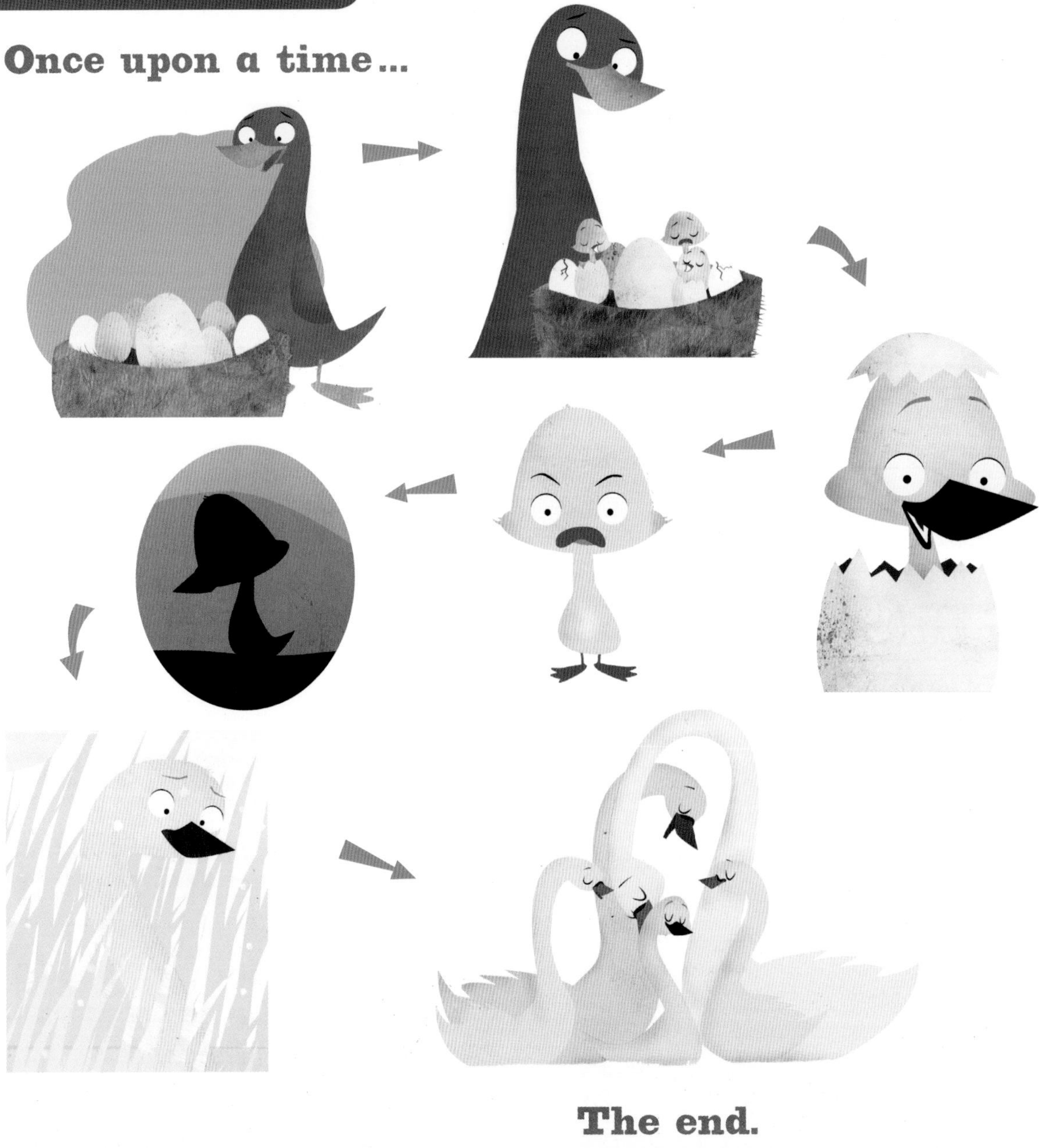

The end.